STILL PRAYING

AFTER ALL THESE YEARS

MEDITATIONS *for* LATER LIFE

SUSAN CAROL SCOTT

UPPER ROOM BOOKS®
NASHVILLE

Still Praying after All These Years: Meditations for Later Life
Copyright © 2019 by Susan Carol Scott
All rights reserved.

Upper Room Books® website: upperroombooks.com

At the time of publication all websites referenced in this book were valid. However, due to the fluid nature of the internet, some addresses may have changed, or the content may no longer be relevant.

Cover design: Juicebox Designs
Interior design: PerfecType | Nashville, TN

Library of Congress Cataloging-in-Publication Data

Names: Scott, Susan C. (Susan Carol), 1946- author.
Title: Still praying after all these years : meditations for later life /
    Susan C. Scott.
Description: [Nashville, TN] : Upper Room Books, [2019] |
Identifiers: LCCN 2018060702 (print) | LCCN 2019010189 (ebook) | ISBN
    9780835818872 (Mobi) | ISBN 9780835818889 (Epub) | ISBN 9780835818865
    (print) | ISBN 9780835818889 (epub.)
Subjects: LCSH: Older people--Prayers and devotions.
Classification: LCC BV4580 (ebook) | LCC BV4580 .S328 2019 (print) | DDC
    242/.65--dc23
LC record available at https://lccn.loc.gov/2018060702

To my father, Wayne, who expressed love by being of use,
and my mother, Betty, who in befriending strangers,
embodied her belief that God is love.

CONTENTS

Acknowledgments 9

Introduction. 11

How to Use This Resource 13

The Meditations

Wherever We Go 16

Expecting Small Miracles. 18

Carry On! 20

Finding New Ways. 22

Checking the Foundations. 24

Can Less Be More?. 26

A Good Listener. 28

That's Good!. 30

Durable and Portable 32

Already . . . Not Yet 34

Love or Nothing 36

Hidden in Plain Sight 38

Is This the Same Person? 40

Desert Grit and Gratitude 42

Medicinal Powers. 44

CONTENTS

New Beginnings. 46

I Love Myself! 48

Quieting the Crazy Things. 50

Worth the Risk?. 52

Quality Living 54

A Winking God. 56

Comfort and Refresh Us 58

Baking a New Beginning. 60

Things We Can Teach 62

Tough and Tender 64

Response of Caring 66

Not Digestible!. 68

Another Day of Fun and Love 70

Sweet Mystery of Life. 72

Seeing God in People's Faces 74

Dread and Delight. 76

The Gift of a Lift 78

Acting for God. 80

Remember Me 82

The Path of Life 84

Sitting with God 86

Up to Me? 88

The School of Life 90

In Our Being 92

Life Worth Living 94

Who's Responsible and Why? 96

CONTENTS

A Lot of Ground to Cover 98

Second-Guessing 100

A Regular Beginner 102

Not Alone 104

Communing 106

Go Ahead and Ask 108

O God, Why? 110

Places of Darkness and Light 112

Where Are You, God? 114

Making Trouble for Each Other 116

Why Am I Here? 118

Scripture Index 121

Notes 125

About the Author 127

ACKNOWLEDGMENTS

I've learned it takes a village to get a book to a publisher's desk. My heartfelt thanks to readers who reflected on early drafts of these meditations: Barbara Pope, Marti Zontek, Rich and Judy Getrich, Marjorie Brown, and my spiritual guide, Rev. Emily Schwenker.

An extra measure of gratitude goes to Rev. Dr. Susan Halverstadt, who kindly arranged to pilot these meditations with some older United Methodist laity in two churches. Their enthusiastic response to that early draft gave me the motivation to forge ahead.

I'm indebted to the following writers for practical help and guidance en route to the door of Upper Room Books: Vinita Hampton Wright; Meredith Sue Willis; Lois Swagerty; Dr. Robert Wicks; Dr. Margaret Benefiel; John Miklos; Rev. Dr. Richard Gentzler; my brother, Don Mitchell; and my daughter, Beth Anne Royer. I was blessed as well with support from my sister, Mary Mitchell; my beloved husband, the late Rev. Dr. Bill; daughter, Carol Royer; and sons Lucas and Jacob Royer. Thank you, dear ones!

I credit a number of gifted clinical pastoral educators and a variety of CPE peers with sharing in my formation (you know who you are). Thank you for teaching me to listen attentively to the aged and my aging self. Particular appreciation goes to the late Dr. Joan Hemenway, esteemed pastoral educator and mentor, for challenging me to write more succinctly. Joan also acquainted me more deeply with the theory and research on human attachment that inform some of these meditations. My gratitude extends to those who modeled contemplative ways of being: my first spouse, the late John F. Royer; dear departed spiritual friend Rev. Dr. Bonnie Brown; staff and peers of Shalem Institute's 2016 Spiritual Guidance Program; and the three gifted women in my locally based spiritual directors' peer group.

Generous in cheering on my creative approaches to holy play with the elderly were Rev. Raymond Cooley, Rev. Anne Baltzell, David Sheehan, and David Bordanaro, all of whom had roles in supporting my ministry in the nursing home world. I also salute the late Rev. David Minnick whose love of holy play with the elderly was happily contagious.

Thanks to so many at Upper Room Books who have been most gracious, encouraging, and patient in helping me learn the ropes of book publishing. In addition, their understanding and kindnesses around the recent and unexpected death of my husband, Bill, will not be forgotten.

INTRODUCTION

This meditation resource is written for older persons going through great changes, some chosen, others unchosen: relocation, health setbacks, loss of mobility, changes in levels of care, loss of valued roles, the death of loved ones. It is also envisioned as a resource for those supporting and caring for elders amid such changes.

Each meditation begins with a thoughtful statement or searching question. These were generated in conversations among elderly participants in a six-week Arts and Spirit group process. While serving as a geriatric chaplain, I led eleven of these groups in nursing homes from 1997 to 2002. Participants ranged in age from 65 to 100 and were of multiple ethnicities and of varied educational, religious, and economic backgrounds.

In these groups, participants used simple musical instruments and movement props to playfully interpret "The Creation," James Weldon Johnson's vivid poetic sermon based on the Genesis creation stories. Discussion followed, exploring themes in the sermon: comfort, loss, suffering, beginnings, loneliness, meaning, purpose, wonder, and God's presence and absence.

The hands-on creative improvisation encouraged in each group session freed participants to give voice to their thoughts and feelings. Often, group members expressed hope that their discussions might be shared with a wider audience. This book of meditations is my way of realizing that hope. These pieces also reflect insights gleaned through one-to-one conversations with nursing home residents. While editing has been done for privacy's sake, I've endeavored to retain the authenticity of their corporate and individual voices. How grateful I am to all those souls who shared their struggles, the prayers of their hearts, and insight of their years! They were teachers to me then, and now, years later, remain valued role models and wisdom figures in my own journey of aging. As they are all most likely now departed, I count these elders as my cosmic cheerleaders. As it says in Hebrews 12:1, "seeing as we are surrounded by so great a cloud of witnesses!"

HOW TO USE THIS
RESOURCE

Readers might engage these meditations on a daily basis for fifty-two consecutive days or marinate in one a week, so they last for an entire year. One advantage of reflecting on one meditation for an entire week is the opportunity for deeper, repeated reflection on a topic and lengthier experimentation with the suggested practice associated with each meditation. Some may find it worthwhile to read the same meditation several times in the same day, as a way of refocusing one's attention on the suggested practice that flows from each reflection. A list of scripture citations is available at the end of the book and may prove helpful not only to readers but also to those who use this book as a resource for ministering with elderly persons in individual encounters or congregational worship.

A Guide to the Format of Each Meditation

Springboard Statements and Questions

Each meditation begins with either a statement or question from an older person living in a congregate care setting. Each passage acts as a springboard for the meditation that follows.

Passage

The selected scripture echoes themes found in the initial statement and/or question and in the Perspective section that follows.

Perspective

This is a reflection on the themes expressed in the initial statement or question as well as the scripture passage.

Practice

The reader is invited to consider a question or undertake an action that may be a form of practicing one's faith. These questions and practices flow from the theme of each meditation.

Prayer

Each prayer is meant to provide an opening to God based on the theme of the meditation and a bridge into everyday living.

The Meditations

Wherever We Go

In making a new beginning, it relaxes me to remember that wherever I go, God is there.

—*Sarah, age 82*

Passage

Where can I go from your spirit?
    Or where can I flee from your presence?
If I ascend to heaven, you are there;
    if I make my bed in Sheol, you are there.
If I take the wings of the morning
    and settle at the farthest limits of the sea,
even there your hand shall lead me,
    and your right hand shall hold me fast.

—Psalm 139:7-10

Perspective

Some of us grew up with "spy-in-the-sky" ideas of God given to us by adults anxious to curb our less civilized behavior. Perhaps those adults hoped an image of a judgmental, all-seeing God would keep us in line until we developed more inner control. Thinking of God this way can make it hard to relax in God's presence. But the idea of God being wherever we are can be relaxing if we understand God's being everywhere as a sign of loving care.

Having been on earth a while, we've likely had brief glimpses of God's presence in a variety of physical and emotional locations, familiar and uncharted. Those glimpses may come by way of others' care or by discovering an unexpected provision for our need. Sometimes, there is simply a deep sense of being led, being one with divine energy, or being held fast in the web of life. In such instances, God is less of a spy-in-the-sky and more of a versatile artist, creating ever-changing ways of making God's holy presence known to us.

Practice

Make a day of noticing some ways God's Spirit is present with both you and others.

Prayer

Holy One, open my eyes to see you, my ears to hear you, and my heart to sense your presence in whatever form you come to me this day.

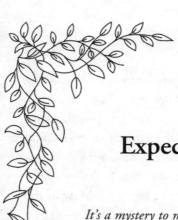

Expecting Small Miracles

It's a mystery to me why things are happening—why they sometimes go the opposite of what I expect. What brings me light in darkness is a small miracle. That's when I don't expect something good to happen and then it does.

—*William, age 84*

Passage

Now faith is the assurance of things hoped for, the conviction of things not seen.

—Hebrews 11:1

Perspective

William realizes that having expectations does not give him control over what actually happens in his life. This awareness leads him to acknowledge the presence of mystery and wonder anew why things happen as they do.

D. W. Winnicott, a child development theorist, suggests that a prerequisite for a dependent child's growth is parental nurture that is "good enough." He suggests that it's not through having his or her needs perfectly met but through reliable care that a child matures. Through "good enough" parenting, a child learns to expect certain outcomes based on past experiences of how his or her parents behaved. In time the child learns that expectations may exceed actual capacity to control what happens.

A child often learns this reality through separations, when access to the parents' presence is temporarily lost, and the child is left with a substitute caregiver. Over numerous experiences of such separations the child learns object constancy—the conviction of things not seen. The child develops a faith that his or her parents continue to exist and care even though they are out of sight. This is how all of us develop both a sense of self as separate from our parents as well as a basic faith in life's goodness, even when reality frustrates our desires.[1]

In this later season of life, our hopes and expectations are sometimes disappointed. At such times, our faith in life's goodness may be shaken. At other times, expecting nothing or anticipating the worst, we are pleasantly surprised by the small miracles that happen to meet our needs. While the world God created isn't entirely our personal oyster, small miracles remind us that God often provides us with enough to survive and, sometimes, with enough to thrive.

Practice

Imagine that a "small miracle" is seeking you out. When it finds you, give thanks.

Prayer

Sustainer of all that is, give me faith that hopes in what I can and cannot see. Thank you for giving me life and for the small miracles that find me each day.

Carry On!

I'm not so much afraid to die, but I am afraid I'll live too long. I'll be glad to make room for someone else on the planet to carry on: carry on with laughter, carry on with helping out children, carry on with bird watching, carry on with enjoying the holidays, carry on with backyard baseball, carry on with it all!

—Adele, age 85

Passage

Let your work be manifest to your servants,
   and your glorious power to their children.
Let the favor of the LORD our God be upon us,
   and prosper for us the work of our hands—
   O prosper the work of our hands!

—Psalm 90:16-17

Perspective

In the second half of life, one of our natural callings is to bless younger generations. We do this by celebrating their gifts, encouraging them to carry on meaningful traditions, and greeting warmly the new ideas and energy they bring to life. If we are currently standing more on the sidelines of a physically active life, we may occasionally feel frustrated. There may also be moments when our thoughts are benevolent and expansive.

Witnessing the pleasure others take in carrying on traditions comes with its own vicarious pleasure. Recalling former delights, we can bless new generations as they carry life forward in the wider world. Offering such blessings is a way to "carry on," for in our own past there were likely elders who blessed us, who saw in our ideas and energy a fresh gift to the earth.

In the end, one of our final gifts is to relinquish the form in which God's life has been expressed in us in order to "make room on the planet" for the life God expresses in new forms.

Practice

Recall persons in your past who blessed you in an undertaking they could no longer venture themselves. Give thanks for their generosity of spirit.

Prayer

Make me a living, breathing blessing. Grant me the grace to make space for your life springing up in forms other than my own.

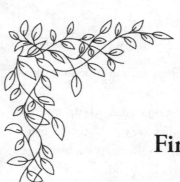

Finding New Ways

When I experience losses and have to find a new way, one thing that helps is thinking of God as the One who wants to give me the strength and help to move forward.

—Harold, age 91

Passage

Jesus said to Thomas, "I am the way, and the truth, and the life."

—John 14:6

Perspective

Some losses remind us of life's impermanence. The inevitability of change is one thing that is guaranteed. In a life full of changes, what is lasting and worthy of our trust?

When a community loses a well-traveled bridge to a flood, motorists who used to cross it search for new ways to get where they're going, routes they otherwise might not have discovered.

Similarly, having suffered a loss, we may eventually sense God's desire for us to move forward. But finding new avenues for our life force may not be as easy as we anticipate. For example, if we've suffered the loss of a physical capacity, how easy it is to forget our new limitation and act as if that bridge is still open. We may be reminded abruptly that our body is no longer capable of what it once was.

When Jesus says, "I am the way," he is letting us know that the route that's always reliably open is the God in whom Jesus put his faith. Our deepest identity is not to be found in all the changing ways we find to get around in this life; rather, it is in our following Jesus' way of trusting God through all our changes. Harold reminds us that in all life's losses, God wants to make a way for us. In trusting this is so, we may be granted "strength and help to move forward" into the Holy Mystery that lies ahead.

Practice

How have you found your way around the washed-out bridges in your life? Where have you felt God's strength and help in moving forward?

Prayer

Way-making God, I will follow your way. Help me to accept my losses and take the time I need to do so. Grant me energy and creativity to find new ways.

Checking the Foundations

I've learned to check my foundations. Wherever I find myself on earth, I'm alert for what isn't substantial. I don't build where it's apt to be dangerous or unsafe. It all goes back to creation. God put things here for us, and they're to be used in a certain way. If I'm not a good steward of what I've been given, then I'm unhappy, and it just doesn't work. It's a good lesson!

—Tom, age 88

Passage

Jesus said, "Everyone then who hears these words of mine and acts on them will be like a wise man who built his house on rock. The rain fell, the floods came, and the winds blew and beat on that house, but it did not fall, because it had been founded on rock. And everyone who hears these words of mine and does not act on them will be like a foolish man who built his house on sand. The rain fell, and the floods came, and the winds blew and beat against that house, and it fell—and great was its fall!"

—Matthew 7:24-27

Perspective

When we worship or make ultimate what is less than God, we're already on shaky ground. When the pressure's on, these lesser gods cannot support the weight of a life.

As Tom observes, when we build on what isn't substantial, then we're apt to misuse the good gifts of the creation and expect more than they can deliver. Then we're disappointed.

The heart of Jesus' teachings is loving God with all our heart, soul, mind, and strength, and loving our neighbor as ourselves. (See Luke 10:27-28.) This is the strong, trusted bedrock on which Jesus advises us to base our lives. Sometimes we only recognize true bedrock after placing our trust in what is less than God. We construct our lives around pleasing others, achieving economic success, the pursuit of perfection, or becoming famous. In time, we discover we never get enough of what we crave. It may be only after a few structural collapses or personal burnouts that we notice God, whose arms are open. God is ready to embrace us in our disillusionment and guide us in building a home on more stable, trustworthy *terra firma*.

Practice

How have outcomes from building on shakier, sandier ground been portals through which you have learned to build on worthier, sturdier foundations?

Prayer

God of all ground, be the bedrock of my life upon which I build in this later season of being.

Can Less Be More?

*God, you've given me so much, but I'm still short on energy. I
can't quite appreciate and do all the things that are thrown at
me. Please, God, give me more energy!*

—Anna, age 79

Passage

Do not cast me off in the time of old age;
 do not forsake me when my strength is spent.

—Psalm 71:9

Perspective

As youngsters at an amusement park, our goal may have been to ride all the
rides. Nowadays, our store of energy may not be equal to the opportunities
that attract us, or even to the things that are thrown at us. When short on
stamina, we're apt to join the psalmist's appeal for more energy. In a society
that rewards overwork and busyness, persons who are short on energy can
imagine themselves less valued. Retirement community slogans stoke those
inadequate feelings with upbeat descriptions of "active aging" and "senior
vitality." If we schedule our lives to prove our continued vigor, we may lose
touch with our body's natural pace at this season.

How might less be more? There is wisdom in accepting that we no longer have the stamina to take on more. Rather than trying to ride all the rides, there is peace to be found in embracing what we can comfortably enjoy. Just as we miss many details of the countryside when speeding, so too, in slowing our pace, we appreciate aspects of life overlooked when we were too busy to notice. When we decelerate, we savor simple activities. We can let ourselves be present more completely to our life and to the lives of others. What a spiritual practice it is to trust that God can do more with our less! What a gift to live with a relaxed and thankful awareness of God with us!

Practice

What rides are you weary of riding? What might you gain in asking less of yourself and in taking on less?

Prayer

O God, in the abundance of your divine economy, do more with my less.

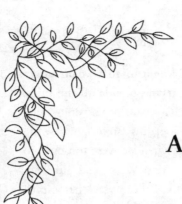

A Good Listener

I had so little time when I used to be the one giving charity, but that changed with age. With that, I never had the time or energy to be much of a doer. But I have had the time to be a good listener!

—Grace, age 84

Passage

You must understand this, my beloved: let everyone be quick to listen, slow to speak, slow to anger.

—James 1:19

Perspective

As we age, time may seem to fly by faster, but we gain time to simply be with others in deeply nourishing ways. We give a true gift in being fully present. While in more active days we measured our charity in numbering our good deeds, now it may be truer that our undivided, kindly attentions feed others' spirits.

To listen well, we temporarily place our desire to be listened to on the back burner. Having two ears and only one mouth, our own anatomy reminds us we were meant to listen twice as much as to talk. As we attend to another's troubles, our memories of facing similar challenges often come to mind. Without rehearsing them aloud, these memories guide us in making supportive comments well-suited to what another shares. We can say we've been in the same boat without turning the spotlight of attention back on our story. We can empathize without offering unwanted advice. Attentive listening is a gift given without strings attached.

In listening attentively to others, we embody how God is fully present to us. Being fully present also reminds us how to open ourselves to listen to God.

Practice

Listen to another today as you wish to be listened to.

Prayer

Listening God, quiet my inner chatter, so I can hear your voice and the voices of my companions.

That's Good!

As I've passed through this life and tried to do what's right, I just hope that, when it's over, God will say to me the same thing God said after completing each day of creating, "That's good!"

—Edgar, age 92

Passage

God saw everything that he had made, and indeed, it was very good. And there was evening and there was morning, the sixth day.

Thus the heavens and the earth were finished, and all their multitude.

—Genesis 1:31–2:1

Perspective

In his poetic sermon entitled "The Creation," James Weldon Johnson vividly reimagines the Genesis creation story. God looks over each day's creation and blesses it with the words: "That's good!"[2] In the Hebrew scriptures, it's reassuring that this initial story of the blessing of all creation precedes the sequel story of our separation from God.

The fresh smell of a baby's skin gives us a bracing whiff of this primal blessing. The poet Wordsworth writes: "Trailing clouds of glory do we come. Heaven lies about us in our infancy."[3] If our aging is a journey toward reunion with our Source, perhaps in approaching our end we'll revisit some of the blessedness of our beginnings.

As we age, we can pray to shed defensive layers—attitudes and behaviors that have separated us from our loving Source. Beneath them lies a treasure: the glory of our original "that's good"-ness. This is the soul, the light placed in us so long ago by our Creator. Thus, we can pray to trail "clouds of glory" not only in our coming but also in our departing.

Practice

Consider what needs to be shed to further uncover soul-light within you.

Prayer

God of all creation, I receive your primal blessing of my being as you say, "That's good!" In receiving that blessing may I glimpse the eternal soul-light in me and in others.

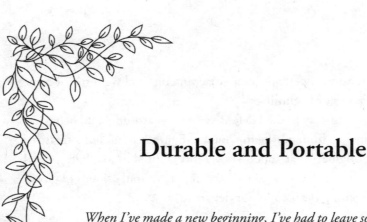

Durable and Portable

When I've made a new beginning, I've had to leave some things behind, but the things I considered to be truly a part of me go with me wherever I go—like dancing, music, or faith.

—Gloria, age 94

Passage

[The Chaldeans] burned the house of God, broke down the wall of Jerusalem, burned all its palaces with fire, and destroyed all its precious vessels. [The king of the Chaldeans] took into exile in Babylon those who had escaped from the sword, and they became servants to him and to his sons until the establishment of the kingdom of Persia.

—2 Chronicles 36:19-20

Perspective

In 586 BCE, the city of Jerusalem was sacked, and the stunned survivors were sent into exile. Not only did their conquerors strip them of many tangible markers of their spiritual identity, but the people also lost the familiar location and context for their lives. What an unwelcome new beginning for the people of Israel!

Through these losses, the people discovered what was durable and portable—what could be taken with them as ongoing resources in their new circumstances. These markers of their identity in God included their shared faith and practice, their memory of sacred texts, prayers, stories, music, and dance. In becoming less dependent on a particular geographical location, they learned to worship God wherever they found themselves.[4]

In imitation of our spiritual ancestors in exile, we can sing a song that reminds us of God's care, recite the poem that speaks peace to us, or recount a story that is food for our soul. Whether we've physically relocated or have gone through other changes, it helps to identify what of our resources are durable and portable and to let these be anchors wherever we find ourselves.

Practice

What resources and markers of your identity in God are an integral part of who you are? What spiritual practices—such as prayer, listening to music, singing, or inspirational reading—might you engage in alone or with others? Identify one and make a habit of it.

Prayer

Everlasting God, thank you for the resources I carry within me, and above all, thank you for your durable, portable, and eternal presence.

Already . . . Not Yet

Being a gracious receiver is hard. Sometimes things are done for me that I'd rather not have done. There's such a difference between the way things are and the way I want them to be. If it were in my power to turn them around, I'd change a few things that are upside down. I'd make things straight and right side up.

—Cecil, age 83

Passage

We know that the whole creation has been groaning in labor pains until now; and not only the creation, but we ourselves, who have the first fruits of the Spirit, groan inwardly while we wait for adoption, the redemption of our bodies. For in hope we were saved. Now hope that is seen is not hope. For who hopes for what is seen? But if we hope for what we do not see, we wait for it with patience.

—Romans 8:22-25

Perspective

As we accept more help from others, the gap between the way things are and the way we want them to be grows wider. When we have more control, we're better able to act to satisfy our preferences. We lose a measure of that control when we accept others' help. One moment we feel grateful for the help, and the next we feel irritated when the helpers' ways of doing things are upside down when their ways are not our ways.

It is a sign of God's life in us to wish that things might be made straight and right side up, to both yearn for some imagined better state of affairs and to change what we can. God is in our groaning discontent and in our work toward what is not yet realized. Nevertheless, the restlessness of this quest can be quieted by an awareness of God in the moment and by gratitude for gifts already at hand. Similarly, God is in our acceptance of and gratitude for what is, but such settled satisfaction sometimes needs to be stirred by holy discontent and longing for a world more in keeping with God's intention.

Practice

Make a spiritual practice of matching every longing thought with a thought of gratitude. Honor both kinds of thoughts as evidence of your God-given humanity.

Prayer

God of my life, help me live gladly and wisely between gratitude for what already is and longing for what has not yet come to pass.

Love or Nothing

I never want to forget that love, real love, is the most important thing. Without love, we're nothing.

—Mary, age 94

Passage

If I speak in the tongues of mortals and of angels, but do not have love, I am a noisy gong or a clanging cymbal. And if I have prophetic powers, and understand all mysteries and all knowledge, and if I have all faith, so as to remove mountains, but do not have love, I am nothing.

—1 Corinthians 13:1-2

Perspective

In his novel *Our Mutual Friend,* Charles Dickens references a popular song lyric of his day: "O, tis love that makes the world go 'round."[5] In the next century, English researcher John Bowlby describes parent-child attachment. He described how separation from the loving nurture of a reliable caregiver fosters anxiety in a child.[6] We may survive without love, but we will not flourish. As a species, giving and receiving love makes our world go around.

In 1 Corinthians 13 Paul puts more value on love than on eloquence, prophetic gifts, an understanding of mysteries, and all knowledge. Why might Paul suggest love is more important than faith? Perhaps because our capacity for faith is shaped by our earliest experiences of receiving and giving love.

Who has been perfectly loved by those who raised us? Our disappointments in how we were loved, and the wounds we bear as a result, invite our trust in the deeper love of God in whom we have our being. We respond to God's gift of love by learning to better love ourselves and one another. We also respond by recognizing how love is being extended to us and by letting that incoming love nourish us.

Practice

Whose love helped you go from being nothing to becoming a cherished someone? How have you played a similar role for others?

Prayer

Lover of my soul, thank you for the affection you have for me and all creation. Grant me an receptive heart that absorbs your love, so that I might freely share that love with my neighbor.

Hidden in Plain Sight

What refreshes me in the desert times in my life? My kindred men and women do. They're often nearby, but I forget to turn to them. It's good that it's in my human nature to feel lonely and need companionship; otherwise, I'd be selfish and think I'm a world unto myself.

—Craig, age 86

Passage

Jesus said, "For where two or three are gathered in my name, I am there among them."

—Matthew 18:20

Perspective

Stranded on a desert island, we would welcome the sight of another human being. Yet, we can live closely with others in families, workplaces, and communities and still behave in ways that keep us stranded and lonely, thinking and acting as if we are a world unto ourselves. In doing so, we overlook the resource of others' presence hidden in plain sight.

We may pride ourselves on the ways we seem independent of others' help, but the underlying truth of our species' existence is that we are more dependent and interdependent than we are independent. None of us survives or flourishes without the support of other persons. We also rely for sustenance on other living entities in the natural world, such as the wide variety of creatures and plant life on which we feed.

If we let them, other people and the Holy Other can refresh us. The presence of others and the Divine Other remind us we are not alone. We are created for companionship, for sharing, and for being of use to one another and the wider creation. When we lend support to one another and work together toward a common goal, what once seemed a desert may bloom and become a place of refreshment for all.

Practice

Whose gift of presence has been hidden in plain sight? How might you serve as an oasis for someone in the desert places of your lives?

Prayer

Holy Other, enlarge the boundaries of my world-unto-myself until it resembles the wideness of your world that encompasses me and so many others.

Is This the Same Person?

Lord, I'm just a spring chicken. I'm only 81. But it's tough when I see things I used to do. I can't even try to do them now. In days gone by, I used to leap out of bed. Now, I ask instead, "Am I the same person?" I wonder a lot about that.

—Daniel, age 81

Passage

You shall love your neighbor as yourself.

—Mark 12:31

Perspective

Are we ever the same person as we were the day before? Likely not. Philadelphia's Franklin Institute once featured a facial time travel exhibit. While looking into the viewer at an image of your face, you turned a dial to watch your face progressively age on a TV screen. It was quite a time-trip!

How ever-changing is our body image across the age spectrum from birth to death's door! Such changes are often so gradual that we're slow to appreciate them from inside our own skin. But we are sure to take notice when our body or brain no longer serves our will as it once did.

As we adjust to changes in our appearance, physical abilities, and mental capacity, we may also undergo an attitude adjustment. When younger and more able-bodied, it was easier to emotionally and physically distance ourselves from the aged or physically challenged. But in time, we may become the one who trips, falls, breaks a bone, and cries out, "How could this have happened?"

These unwelcome calamities collapse the distance between "us" and "them." In accepting a more vulnerable self-image, our empathy grows for those we once identified as "them." "Them" becomes "us," and at once our heart goes out to others and to ourselves.

Practice

How have your own troubles sensitized you toward the troubles of others? Put that sensitivity to use by reaching out to someone you once avoided due to his or her infirmities.

Prayer

God of my ever-changing life, teach me to love myself just as I am, so I might love others just as they are.

Desert Grit and Gratitude

One resource I've discovered for dealing with the desert places in my life is expressing gratitude. A long time ago I learned to pray and thank God for everything I have.

—Helen, age 95

Passage

Give thanks in all circumstances; for this is the will of God in Christ Jesus for you.

—1 Thessalonians 5:18

Perspective

Something about being in arid, gritty, desert lands heightens our gratitude for any small creature comfort we happen upon—the shade of a palm tree, an outcrop of rock sheltering us from windblown sand, or the oasis whose cool slippery waters quench our thirst. Extreme environments have a way of bringing us back to basics. They put us in touch with our human fragility, increasing our appreciation for resources that keep us alive.

Habits of prayer and thanksgiving are also survival resources when we find ourselves in a stripped-down, desert-like life situation. Such habits invite us to notice things we might otherwise overlook, resources that are contributing to our well-being. Those who keep a daily gratitude journal often report an overall improvement in attitude. They begin to notice the provisions for their lives that they once took for granted. While giving thanks in all things may seem an impossible expectation, sometimes a tall order like that one moves us a little further down the road to a truly grateful heart.

Practice

Throughout the day, write down a few things for which you find yourself grateful. Before going to bed, read your list back to yourself. Notice how your body feels when it's in a thankful mode.

Prayer

Giving God, grow my gratitude in plenty and in extremity. For the many ways you supply my body and spirit, thanks!

Medicinal Powers

When I look out the window and gaze at the landscape, it makes me relax. The view has medicinal powers. Nature is my healer.

—Clara, age 96

Passage

The heavens are telling the glory of God;
 and the firmament proclaims his handiwork.
Day to day pours forth speech,
 and night to night declares knowledge.

—Psalm 19:1-2

Perspective

As children, we were attracted to the out-of-doors. We may have had a tree under whose spreading canopy we found comfort. Perhaps there were hills we climbed to test our bodies and gain perspective. Nearby streams may have beckoned us to sit and dream. Repairing to a special spot in nature that seems ours alone is a way of soothing and renewing our soul when we are worried or troubled.

Like God, the natural world is more than the backdrop of our life. We participate in and belong to it, even as it sustains us. Rushing headlong into the future can put us out of touch with nature and separate us from nature's Source. Just as a child in difficulty seeks out a nurturing parent in time of crisis, so we seek the solace of the natural world when life events stop us in our tracks.

We never outgrow this need for contact with the created world, even if we are limited to looking out the window at our surroundings. Our relationship with God and the natural world is of a piece. When communing with God through creation, our illusions of independence and separation can be healed. In this communion we embrace the deep truths of our dependence on God and interdependence with other life forms. The natural world of God's creation has medicinal powers!

Practice

Whether it's getting out of doors or simply looking out the window of a car, a home, or a building, spend a few moments taking in the healing power of God's creation.

Prayer

God of natural wonders, sensing your presence in all you've created, I ask for your healing in the most essential ways.

New Beginnings

For me, some new beginnings have been a nightmare. I've found it hard to make major adjustments. Even so, I've sometimes discovered that a new beginning can hold unexpected, positive possibilities.

—Jeremy, age 77

Passage

Do not remember the former things, or consider the things of old. I am about to do a new thing; now it springs forth, do you not perceive it? I will make a way in the wilderness and rivers in the desert.

—Isaiah 43:18-19

Perspective

New beginnings are a mixed bag. We may feel two ways about the unfamiliar, feeling both anxious and excited. It's natural to be drawn to what is known and to be wary of uncharted territory. Our curiosity and sense of adventure help to overcome our resistance to what is new to us.

Isaiah writes these words about not remembering former things to a people who'd been ripped out of their homeland and carted off to the kingdom of Babylon. Mired in grief over what they'd lost and anxious about the uncertainties of their new situation, they likely drew comfort from nostalgically recalling their former life. How difficult it must have been for them to trust in God's continuing care while in exile! Perhaps Isaiah's message sparked their curiosity about what God might be up to in their stressful situation.

As we age, changes are apt to rock our boat more than in the past. It can take longer to adapt and get our sea legs. Though building trust in unfamiliar circumstances takes time, God meets us and loves us through both our resistance and receptivity to strange new beginnings. Changes activate our curiosity about how God may be at work in our circumstances. Changes also challenge us to become creative meaning-makers in our new circumstances. In this way we collaborate with God in making a way in the wilderness.

Practice

What are some ways you've made it through other changes in your life with the help of God and others? How is the knowledge of your past experiences in exile a resource for you in your current situation?

Prayer

Holy One, may I witness your activity in what is tried and true and in what is strange and new.

I Love Myself!

It has taken a long time for me to love myself. But recently I can say, "I love myself!" It's great! I like me! I am whatever I am with God's help, and it's alright for me to love myself because God made me. I accepted God's love, so I could love.

—Betty, age 96

Passage

No one has ever seen God; if we love one another, God lives in us, and his love is perfected in us. So we have known and believe the love that God has for us. . . .God is love, and those who abide in love abide in God, and God abides in them.

—1 John 4:12, 16

Perspective

In these joyous words, Betty celebrates her growing capacity to love herself. As a young woman, she celebrated her daring as a wing walker; she stood on the wings of a biplane while it was in flight. Now she celebrates that she can finally nest her own self-love within her identity as one of God's valued creations. In accepting God's love, she is empowered to love not only herself but also others.

In saying, "Love your neighbor as yourself," Jesus makes clear that love of self creates optimal conditions for extending genuine, unconditional love to others. (See Mark 12:30-31.) We learn to love ourselves through persons who embody God's love for us, teaching us we are lovable. In time, we notice that, having internalized their love, their love sustains us even when they are not physically present. This sets us on a lifetime path of learning to love ourselves and others. Could it be that a loving, unseen Presence brings all creation into being, sustains it, and receives it back? Each new day presents us with new occasions to trust that this is so.

Practice

Recall a few people in your life who taught you that you were lovable. Look in a mirror and say out loud: "God loves me! I love me!" Complete the circle of love by reaching out in love to someone else.

Prayer

God, when struggling to love myself, remind me I am ever held in your embrace. At the last, may my self-love be totally nested in your love.

Quieting the Crazy Things

I say my prayers, and sometimes I say them a couple of times over. It means a great deal to me. It helps the time go by, and it's better than thinking of crazy things.

—Madge, age 85

Passage

Be still, and know that I am God!
    I am exalted among the nations,
    I am exalted in the earth.

—Psalm 46:10

Perspective

Prayer and meditation can be a powerful prescription for restless minds. While our minds are useful tools for making our way in the world, they are not all of who we are. When we fear for our future and are in touch with what we can't control, the mind can spin its wheels, "thinking a lot of crazy things." Silent meditators call this experience "monkey mind."

Prayer invites us to be present to what is. In prayer we can witness our thoughts and quiet our mind's anxiety. In prayer we root our being in our deepest identity as a beloved of God. This grants us a measure of inner steadiness.

Prayer's portable sanctuary can go with us into whatever, whenever, and wherever. We need only be willing to enter that spacious place within. God meets us there. We can bring with us our worries about what comes next, unburden ourselves, and listen for the whisper of divine guidance.

Practice

Be a witness to your mind's monkey business and remind yourself that you are much more than your mind; you are one of God's beloved.

Prayer

Holy God, quiet the thoughts that give me no peace and draw me into the quieter sanctuary you have placed within me.

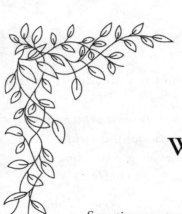

Worth the Risk?

Sometimes a stranger provides companionship, so I will stop and chat for a few minutes. In the past, I had some wonderful companions. We enjoyed good times together. Then one after the other, they all died. I ask myself: Is it worth the risk to get close to someone, only to lose them?

—Bud, age 89

Passage

Jesus said, "Blessed are those who mourn, for they will be comforted."
—Matthew 5:4

Perspective

We grow accustomed to beloved companions who play their signature tunes on our heartstrings. When persons dear to us die, we deeply miss their particular melodies. In grief, it's natural for our heart's instrument to lie silent awhile. Silence honors the gift that persons were to the world and to us.[7]

The pain of grief may make us think twice about giving our heart again. In later years, statistical chances are higher that we'll suffer the loss of a peer we've newly embraced. Knowing this, we may seriously weigh whether it's "worth the risk" to become attached again, either in a close friendship or in an intimate partnership.

In time we may feel ready to seek out new companions who make our heart sing. If we find a special someone, we can still continue to cherish our relationship with our deceased loved ones. In meeting our need for friendship, we may also meet another's similar need. The gift goes both ways. In Genesis, God creates a second human after deciding it's not good for Adam to be alone. (See Genesis 2:18.) The creation story in Genesis suggests we were created to be in mutual relationship. It is a mark of our humanity.

Practice

Whether by phone, mail, or in person, move out of your comfort zone to express friendly interest in someone who is relatively unknown to you. If the person seems receptive, also risk sharing something about yourself that might help the person know you better.

Prayer

Bless the ongoing communion I enjoy with those I love who are no longer physically present. Should the right opportunity present itself, grant me the courage to risk new, nourishing relationships.

Quality Living

God, you appreciate my efforts even when I fail. Truly, I have
to fail and know what it is to lose things in order to be successful
in the quality of my living.

—*Marguerite, age 92*

Passage

So teach us to count our days
　　that we may gain a wise heart.

—Psalm 90:12

Perspective

Who among us wishes to experience failure and loss? Would we trust a God who would zap us with losses and failures just to teach us lessons? Failure and loss happen to us all, and we have a choice of how to respond. In his book *Man's Search for Meaning*, Viktor Frankl observes that, although concentration camp prisoners were stripped of many things, one thing they could not be robbed of was their choice of how to respond to what befell them.[8]

At worst, we can let failure and loss leave us permanently guarded and bitter. At best, we can allow such experiences to transform us into wiser, more compassionate human beings. Life may have dealt us a difficult hand of cards, yet we can still play them as best as we know how.

Failure teaches us about our weaknesses and the limits of our power. Loss bids us value the treasure of the here and now, heightening our awareness of the precious moments in which we live. As Marguerite so wisely reminds us, the quality of our days can be shaped beneficially by how we respond to failure and loss. Some of God's best work in us is done in the wake of unwelcome events.

Practice

Think of a loss or failure you've suffered and consider how your response to it has positively or negatively affected the quality of your living. Is there a way to change how you interpret that event and thus change your response?

Prayer

Healing God, I offer you my bitterness and my yearning to be free of resentment. Use them in the service of my transformation.

A Winking God

God, you must have a sense of humor. I see you winking at me.
—Anabelle, age 87

Passage

A cheerful heart is a good medicine,
  but a downcast spirit dries up the bones.

—Proverbs 17:22

Perspective

Holy humor leaves us lightened up, less grim, and more happily connected to each other. If you are a natural sobersides, it may challenge you to imagine God's winking eye in everyday exasperations. Some of the best humor springs from our experience of being out of control as our best-laid plans upend, our overblown egos puncture, or our awkwardness makes us uncomfortable.

Even some of aging's limitations provide us a momentary chuckle. Hearing difficulties create exasperation for hearing-impaired persons and those trying to communicate with that person. But within that frustration may come a gracious moment when both parties chuckle over the disconnect between what was actually said and what the hearing-impaired persons thought they heard. Then mutual laughter blessedly dissipates shared aggravation.

It's no wonder we are drawn to someone who is blessed with a sense of humor. The best humor grants us fresh perspectives on what's most important and what's small stuff. Belly laughing in the same boat can be more fun than sailing off sullenly in separate skiffs.[9] A good laugh with a winking God and with one another is a great way to start the day.

Practice

Experiment with lightening up an everyday bodily annoyance with laughter. Imagine a winking God who is laughing with you.

Prayer

Winking God, may I hear your holy laughter today when I need it most.

Comfort and Refresh Us

Your ordinary ways and your mysterious ways comfort and refresh me, O God.

—*Sam, age 90*

Passage

The LORD is my shepherd, I shall not want.
　　He makes me lie down in green pastures;
he leads me beside still waters;
　　he restores my soul.
He leads me in right paths
　　for his name's sake.

—Psalm 23:1-3

Perspective

God's ordinary ways are made visible in everyday miracles. These miracles include intentional patterns of nurture and labor that weave the fabric of family and community life.[10] In cooperative patterns of routine and rest, we find a welcome in creature comforts. In such patterns lie gifts often unacknowledged.

When life is stripped down to the essentials, things we once took for granted can go a long way to refresh us. We find green pastures and still waters in the solace of another's warm smile, a kindly hand on our shoulder, the provision of a meal we didn't have to cook, the comfort of clean sheets, the refreshment of a shower, or the availability of compassionate helpers.

Our soul's thirst is also quenched by mystery—by happenings that fall outside our habitual expectations: the spontaneous act of sacrificial love, inexplicable courage in the face of great odds, or gracious happenstance that opens a door to a new relationship or endeavor. No matter our life situation, God's ordinary and mysterious ways sustain us in good times and bad.

Practice

Today, look for how God might be comforting and refreshing you in ordinary ways and in mysterious ways.

Prayer

O God, give me eyes to see your comfort and refreshment made visible this day.

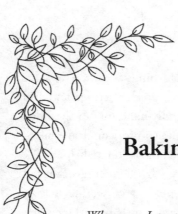

Baking a New Beginning

Whenever I prepared to bake a loaf of bread, it was a new beginning of a sort. I'd start with flour, eggs, and yeast, and end up with something that didn't look at all like any of the ingredients with which I'd started. In baking bread, I had to rely on the power of the yeast. The power I've relied on in making any new beginning is willpower. Willpower helps me get through it, and so does God.

—*Walter, age 83*

Passage

For the one who sanctifies and those who are sanctified all have one Father. For this reason Jesus is not ashamed to call them brothers and sisters.

—Hebrews 2:11

Perspective

Walter, who'd made his living as a baker, compared the ingredients of bread to the act of making a new start. Just as a baker needs yeast to make bread, we need human willpower inspired by God.

A church council in 451 CE decided to represent Jesus Christ's nature as being both fully human and fully divine.[11] The creative tension in this doctrine honors both the reality of Jesus' God-given humanity and the activity of God in him that made him a faithful image of his Divine Parent. Our ancestors in faith thought emphasizing one without the other promoted a half-truth. Like the power of yeast, this chemistry of humanity and divinity is what makes Jesus Christ wholly who he is.

In Christian scripture, Jesus refers to his disciples as siblings (see Matthew 12:46-50), while in the Hebrew scriptures we're told we are made in God's image (see Genesis 1:26). This suggests that we too live in creative tension between being human creatures who possess a will and being creatures who reflect divine life. Our God-given willpower and God-energy at work outside us helps us get through new challenges. The creative tension between the two is a yeasty mix that helps make a risen-loaf of a life, as God intends.

Practice

How is God at work in your exercise of willpower? Where do you notice God's activity outside your exercise of will?

Prayer

May your divine life, expressed in my humanity, be the yeasty mix that creates a risen-loaf life. Make me your bread, fit to nourish others.

Things We Can Teach

Perhaps in this season of life I am a teacher, and there are still things that I can teach.

—Katherine, age 86

Passage

Hear, my child, your father's instruction,
    and do not reject your mother's teaching;
for they are a fair garland for your head,
    and pendants for your neck.

—Proverbs 1:8-9

Perspective

Though in life's later season we may not preside over a classroom, yet perhaps we are still teachers. Medical personnel sharpen their caregiving skills with the feedback we provide. A peer who is struggling to adjust to a new bodily limitation takes heart in noticing how we've learned to live with a similar challenge. When asked, we share insights and perspectives honed over many years on the planet.

In this later season of life, do we find ourselves with greater empathy for departed loved ones whose aging we witnessed? Now that we're dealing with some of the daily burdens and stresses of living in an aging body, we can better understand why they were sometimes out of sorts and short-tempered with others. With this newfound insight we can extend compassion to our aging selves when we are feeling anxious, impatient, or just plain grumpy.

We too are role models for younger members of our extended family who will someday grow old. By just being in our presence, they learn about meeting the challenges of aging with grace, spunk, and generosity of spirit. Our behavior may not always be beyond reproach, especially on days when we are feeling exasperated by the ways our body struggles or demands more care. Nevertheless, we can teach others through the witness of our living—how we face the unknowns and walk by faith, not by sight.

Practice

Name some ways in which are you a stealth teacher to others at this time in your life.

Prayer

O God, may all who are taught by the witness of my life learn more of you and your faithfulness.

Tough and Tender

Life is hard for me, but I'm not alone in that. While life is good, life is also tough.

—*Stewart, age 95*

Passage

I will give them one heart, and put a new spirit within them; I will remove the heart of stone from their flesh and give them a heart of flesh, so that they may follow my statutes and keep my ordinances and obey them. Then they shall be my people, and I will be their God.

—Ezekiel 11:19-20

Perspective

This passage suggests that a pliable "heart of flesh" unites us with God and with one another as God's people. Recent heart research suggests the human heart has a mind of its own. It influences how we see and interpret events and communicates its perspective to the brain.[12]

Being human comes with its share of welcome blessings and tough realities. Our personal circumstances may be challenging, yet we can still have a heart for others' difficulties. As we age, our spiritual heart may expand and grow more tender, even as our personal world contracts. The rich and varied experiences we've had over the arc of our lives help us experience with empathy the joys and sorrows of others. Our experiences also cause us to be deeply moved by the agonies and ecstasies of earth, our home.

Helpers for seniors are sometimes new to this country while others are folks who work several jobs to make ends meet or young people taking on adult responsibilities. We can't relieve the burdens of those hired to help us, but we can be caring listeners and encourage their hopes and dreams. In listening to caregivers, we affirm their worth and enlarge our own world. We might learn about a country we've never visited or be introduced to a new technology that excites the younger generation. By showing interest in caregivers and having a tender heart for their challenges, we create a connecting bridge across the gap between our life situation and theirs. Bringing a tender "heart of flesh" to these encounters wakens us to the recognition that we are soul siblings in God's family.

Practice

Recall encouraging words said to you by a family member, friend, or stranger who lent you support when you were in a tough situation. Today, let your softness of heart find a way to pay that kindness forward to someone else.

Prayer

O God, when the going gets tough, make my heart more tender.

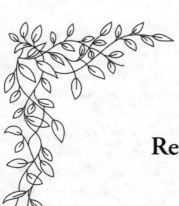

Response of Caring

I long for the responsibility of having others to care for. Some-
times I make my way down the hall and stop to talk with people
who are suffering. My talking with them seems to suffice. It's
nothing I plan. I put my hand on a shoulder to give comfort. I
get more out of it than they do. God, I am thankful I can help
someone else, and that we can be helpful to one another.

—*Edward, age 70*

Passage

A leper came to Jesus begging him, and kneeling he said to him, "If you
choose, you can make me clean." Moved with pity, Jesus stretched out his
hand and touched him, and said to him, "I do choose. Be made clean!"

—Mark 1:40-41

Perspective

Two root words form the word responsibility—*response* and *ability*. Offering comfort to a suffering person is evidence of our ability to respond sen-
sitively to another's plight. Giving comfort can be as simple as the outreach
Ed describes, and it is akin to how Jesus ministers to persons. Accepting
their worth and wounds, Jesus conveys his care by listening attentively and

responding compassionately. His response often includes tender and appropriate physical touch. In this age of advanced medical technology, there are still physicians who understand that simple human touch has a healing power all its own.

We get a lot out of making a positive difference for others. Those who graciously receive our care give us the gift of purposeful activity. Givers may feel more powerful in their role than receivers, yet caregivers do well to remember that tomorrow, they too may have need to receive the very same gift of care they offer today. With that in mind, we can offer our gifts free of a false sense of superiority. How blessed we are to share in the rhythms of giving and receiving.

Practice

Find an opportunity to use your ability to respond by imitating Jesus' caring way of being with persons. Consider both the gift you receive from those who accept your care and the gift you give in receiving others' care for you.

Prayer

Enliven me through the gifts I receive in giving care and the gifts I give in receiving others' care. Before you I will dance to these alternating rhythms of giving and receiving.

Not Digestible!

My spouse worked in the oyster industry, and from him I learned that the oyster makes the pearl. In the Japanese oyster industry, a little grain of sand is inserted in each oyster. It irritates the oyster, causing it to form pearly layers around the grain of sand. The oyster makes the pearl from a grain of sand—from something that's not digestible.

—Claudia, age 91

Passage

Jesus said, "Again, the kingdom of heaven is like a merchant in search of fine pearls; on finding one pearl of great value, he went and sold all that he had and bought it."

—Matthew 13:45-46

Perspective

Our spiritual growth can be furthered by that which initially seems indigestible. When the Hebrew people wander in the desert, they are in dire need of nourishment. In Exodus 16:13-21, we read how each morning, God provides an edible substance on the desert floor—the sweet excrement of two insects. Is it any wonder the people question whether it is digestible?

They call it manna, meaning in Hebrew: "What is it?"[13] They cannot hoard or store this foodstuff. Through it, they learn to trust God's daily provision. What first seems to be an indigestible grain of sand proves to be a valuable spiritual pearl.

As we age, experiences may befall us that we find indigestible—some so unpalatable that they actually affect our digestion. Living alone for the first time, learning to live without a car, paying someone to care for us in our home, leaving a beloved home for a congregate living situation, being obliged to use a cane, walker, or wheelchair are just a few grains of sand that irritate one's personal oyster. Perhaps not all grains of sand in our lives can be appreciated as valuable pearls, but we may find a few grains around which layers of spiritual meaning can be deposited. These "pearls" may prove to be hidden gems of God's design.

Practice

Name the most irritating grains of sand in your personal oyster. Which do you think might have the potential to become spiritually valuable to you in some way?

Prayer

Providing God, may the layers of meaning I create around some of life's hardships produce pearls that are of value in your divine realm.

Another Day of Fun and Love

O God, make my day come in the morning. Bring me through
the night and give me another day to live—another day of fun
and love. Thank you for another day, bright and early.

—*Wilma, age 86*

Passage

Turn, O Lord! How long?
    Have compassion on your servants!
Satisfy us in the morning with your steadfast love,
    so that we may rejoice and be glad all our days.

—Psalm 90:13-14

Perspective

When we take for granted each new day, viewing it as a deserved entitlement, we lose sight of the gift of life. When we view the day as a gift to unwrap with curious anticipation, we enter it with a more open spirit—a willingness to let it unfold. The lens through which we look at each new day can affect how we interpret our experiences.

One of the historic catechisms of the Christian church, the Westminster Shorter Catechism, suggests that the chief purpose of humans is "to glorify God, and to enjoy [God] forever."[14] This sounds downright play-ful! Yet how often do we envision our relationship with God as enjoyable? Maybe we have been too somber and serious, while our real call is to take delight in being one of God's beloveds. The words of this catechism can be heard as God's daily invitation to buoyancy—to receive the gift of another day of fun and love.

Practice

How does what you look for in each new day affect what you tend to notice? How does what you expect shape how you interpret and experience the hap-penings of that day?

Prayer

Thank you for the miracle of each new day I am given. Help me find something to playfully enjoy in the gift of this day.

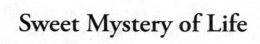

Sweet Mystery of Life

Up in the night sky I see a streak of light. What could it be? The Milky Way? A comet? There are things in the sky that come and go, that make me ask, "Where did it go, and why did it come back?" So many mysteries! It makes me wonder about lots of things—like how much of today goes back to the beginning? "Ah! Sweet mystery of life!"[15]

—*Murray, age 89*

Passage

God made the two great lights—the greater light to rule the day and the lesser light to rule the night—and the stars. God set them in the dome of the sky to give light upon the earth, to rule over the day and over the night, and to separate the light from the darkness. And God saw that it was good. And there was evening and there was morning, the fourth day.

—Genesis 1:16-19

Perspective

Murray's exclamation of wonder was evoked by the appearance of the Hale-Bopp comet in the spring of 1997. This comet last entered our solar system in 2215 BCE and will not return until the year 4525 CE.[16] Murray knew this cosmic event would not be repeated in his lifetime. This knowledge only enriched his sense of awe that this comet had come around while he was alive to behold it.

In visiting an awesome natural wonder in our youth, we may have soothed our regrets about leaving by vowing to return someday. As our future is foreshortened by age, we realize some peak experiences may not be repeatable in our lifetime. While this may disappoint, it also heightens our attentiveness to what we are privileged to experience. Life's time limits deepen our appreciation of the present and its precious, unrepeatable nature. Enraptured by wonder, we momentarily forget ourselves and are caught up in a divine mystery more timeless than our short, mortal lives. What holy ground!

Practice

As you go through your day, find reasons and occasions to say with Murray: "Ah! Sweet mystery of life!"

Prayer

God of the universe, when beholding your creation, all I can say is "Wow!" Attune my ears to the celestial songs of genomes and galaxies, and in that music let me hear your voice.

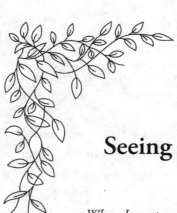

Seeing God in People's Faces

When I meet someone for the first time, I look at them, and
they look at me. What helps me make a new beginning is seeing
God in people's faces.

—*Clarence, age 82*

Passage

Jacob said, "No, please; if I find favor with you, then accept my present from
my hand; for truly to see your face is like seeing the face of God—since you
have received me with such favor."

—Genesis 33:10

Perspective

After living elsewhere, Jacob risks returning home to face his fraternal twin,
Esau. Years before, Jacob cheated Esau out of his birthright. Jacob now longs
to be reconciled, but he isn't sure if Esau's rage has cooled in the interim.
Nevertheless, Jacob risks the reunion and learns that Esau is open to restor-
ing their relationship. This makes it possible for them to relate to each other
in more life-giving ways. Jacob acknowledges this when they meet, saying to
Esau: "to see your face is like seeing the face of God." It's as if Jacob is truly
seeing his brother for the first time.

It's easy to stay on a superficial level with someone new when we only have passing contact with him or her. Yet it's also possible to have regular contact with someone for years but not truly meet each other. It may take a change of heart on our part before we can look into each other's eyes and truly engage in a meaningful way. When we risk letting ourselves be known to each other on a deeper level, it changes us and a new relationship begins. It's as if we see the face of God in each other.

Practice

With whom might you make a new beginning by changing your attitude toward that person and your relationship with him or her? How might you begin that change?

Prayer

May I ever seek and find your face, O God. In facing you, let me see your face in those around me.

Dread and Delight

How many times do I wake up and say: "O God, not another day like this! What's going to happen next?" Though I never know what I might go through in a whole day, still, I thank you for it.

—*Bernice, age 75*

Passage

This is the day that the LORD has made;
let us rejoice and be glad in it.

—Psalm 118:24

Perspective

Each day is like a little life that dawns with our rising and ends as we drift into sleep. As we greet a new day with thanks, we know an entire day may hold some things we dislike. Asking for God's help in meeting those unwelcome happenings is a fine place to begin.

No matter the feelings that arise in us about what happens, we can accept and move through those feelings. No matter how limited our options, we can choose our outward response to what's outside our power to control. Even if we act on our feelings in ways we later regret, God can redeem those

76

acts through our healthy remorse and honest confession. We cooperate with God's redemptive agenda by accepting ourselves as forgiven and by reflecting on how we might respond more resourcefully in the future. Thus, through steps and missteps, we can let God's Spirit transform us.

To be a more faithful reflection of God's loving presence, we learn to act on our feelings in ways that are resourceful, respectful, and redemptive. While taking this challenge seriously, we need not approach it grimly. We can engage some of what we dread with a spirit of improvisation and curiosity. Imagining God as our playful coconspirator, perhaps we can transform a daily dread into an unexpected opportunity for delight.

Practice

Imagine how God might be inviting you to join in some redemptive playfulness by responding creatively to something you dislike or dread. When you act on what you've imagined, think of it as you and God engaging in some holy play.

Prayer

God of delight, between my rising and my resting, be with me in my responding.

The Gift of a Lift

What gives me a lift are the sayings I live with. I used to be a church clerk. I'd read something in the church newsletter, and if I liked it, I'd save it and commit it to memory. Here's one I remember that's a Chinese proverb: "Life itself can't give you joy unless you really will it. Life just gives you time and space, it's up to you to fill it!"

—Florence, age 99

Passage

He gives power to the faint,
    and strengthens the powerless.
Even youths will faint and be weary,
    and the young will fall exhausted;
but those who wait for the Lord shall renew their strength,
    they shall mount up with wings like eagles,
they shall run and not be weary,
    they shall walk and not faint.

—Isaiah 40:29-31

Perspective

The airfoil shape of an eagle's wings helps give it the lift to gain altitude. This shape causes air to flow faster over the upper surface of its wings, and the eagle rises.[17] When our spirits need a lift, we create an airfoil of sorts by engaging in what brings us comfort and perspective to help us rise.

The knowledge of what boosts our spirits may be hard-won over a lifetime. Florence, a former church clerk, knew the lift she got from certain sage sayings. With her vision failing, she continued to draw inspiration from these nuggets of wisdom that she'd committed to memory. Though we intentionally identify and use such spirit-lifting resources to help ourselves, we can still experience their benefits as a gift. Our capacity to draw on resources that soothe and elevate our spirits is God-given.

But there are also limits to what we can offer ourselves—times when none of the tried and true approaches seem sufficient to our need. Sometimes we can only wait in hope on the provision of a holy energy that seems beyond our own to give us the lift for which we hunger.

Practice

How do you give yourself a lift? When have you sensed a need for the divine provision of strength beyond your known resources? How did that provision come?

Prayer

Thanks be to God for the gift of a lift in every breath I take.
When my resources are spent, O God, I await replenishment
by the infilling of your
Holy Spirit.

Acting for God

Many people have faith in God, including me. I recognize that God exists, but my interpretation of who God is may differ from that of someone else. I can call on God for help, but it's not going to be a tit-for-tat deal. Still, I go ahead and ask for divine help and act for God when no other help is around.

—Chuck, age 87

Passage

[God] is not far from each one of us. For "In him we live and move and have our being"; as even some of your own poets have said, "For we too are his offspring."

—Acts 17:27-28

Perspective

As Chuck reminds us, our relationship with God is not an "I'll scratch your back, you'll scratch mine" deal. Our relationship might be better described as "hand-in-glove." When aligned with God's loving, creative purposes, God is the animating hand in the glove of our life. Still, as one person, we are each but one expression of God's life in the world and are never the sum total of God's being or doing. Thus, there are times when we call out for help from the One in whose larger life we participate.

An oft-used sermon illustration tells of a man who arrived in heaven after being swept off his roof by flood waters. He complained that his many prayers for rescue had been unanswered. God replied that help had been offered to him three times. The distressed man had refused to recognize the neighbor in the inflatable raft, the rescuer in the canoe, and the police officer in a motor boat as God's response to his plight.

God's answer to our cries sometimes comes in the form of others' outreach. At other times, it is we who "act for God" in responding to a needful situation. Thus, in all of us, the loving nature of our Creator finds animation, and we become expressions of God's life in this world.

Practice

Today, make yourself available to be used by God as an agent of lovingkindness. Be alert for moments when God's helping hand is being extended to you through another.

Prayer

Be the animating hand in the glove of my life, O God. Give me eyes to recognize your care, alive in the extended hands of others.

Remember Me

Here's one thing I've lost as I've aged. I've lost my memory. It's just not there! Sometimes I have to say, "I'm sorry. I'd like to remember, but I can't." What helps me get through this loss is imagining God as the One who remembers me and gives me the strength to move forward.

—Terrence, age 68

Passage

But Zion said, "The LORD has forsaken me,
    my Lord has forgotten me."
Can a woman forget her nursing child,
    or show no compassion for the child of her womb?
Even these may forget,
    yet I will not forget you.
See, I have inscribed you on the palms of my hands;
    your walls are continually before me.

—Isaiah 49:14-16

Perspective

From the moment of our birth, our survival depends on our caregivers' capacity to both remember us and keep in mind our need for care. As we mature, our growing ability to remember grants us a sense of mastery and a capacity to cultivate relationships. No wonder it's so frustrating in later life to struggle to remember.

While cognitive losses bring grief, they also bring some forms of relief. We might get a brief taste of what Søren Kierkegaard calls "the eternal in the present moment."[18] In the eternal present, fresh wonder and gratitude walk hand in hand. Living more in the moment, we may be blessedly relieved when our mind no longer latches onto past regrets or nurses old grudges. We also may worry less about what comes next.

When being a mental retriever gets harder, becoming a willing receiver is a gracious and resourceful way to respond. Accepting our need to be dependent in some matters can be the best demonstration of our maturity and responsibility. Sometimes this entails relying on trusted others whose memories and minds function better than ours. This is an exercise in faith, akin to trusting God. Whether or not there are gaps in our memory, how reassuring it is to be loved by a God who assures us that we will not be forgotten, and that we'll be inscribed on the very palms of God's hands.

Practice

Whether or not you have memory issues, spend some time in the eternal present today and see what surprises and blesses you.

Prayer

Remember me, O God! Keep me in mind even when I forget you.

The Path of Life

*God, why did it take so long for me to understand a little bit
more about you? You are love. You lead me on the path of life.*
—*Isabelle, age 87*

Passage

You show me the path of life.
    In your presence there is fullness of joy;
    in your right hand are pleasures forevermore.

—Psalm 16:11

Perspective

Life is often compared to a path. A sixth-century Roman Christian named
Boethius speaks this way about how God is the path of life:

To see Thee is the end and the beginning.
Thou carriest us and thou dost go before.
Thou art the journey and the journey's end.[19]

On life's path we take a long and sometimes wandering journey toward
appreciating how inseparable God and love are. Twice the fourth chapter of
John's first epistle simply declares: God is love. (See 1 John 4:8, 16.)

This understanding of the equivalence between love and God is not head learning as much as it is experiential learning—a heart wisdom that develops through walking life's path. This wisdom gets under our skin and into the very fiber of our being. How memorable is this form of learning! It has a way of transforming us and how we see the world. We come to see all the varied forms of the created world as ways in which God's love is being made manifest. We also sense how our human fears and need for control distort the image of God's love that each of us is created to be.

Practice

Today, on your path of life, be open to new understandings about the connection between God and love. When you notice the connection, give thanks.

Prayer

O God, you are my journey—its beginning, middle, and end. Whether I walk, skip, or shuffle along the road, may it lead me to a home in your love.

Sitting with God

Good and bad, that's how life comes. Yes, there's good and bad, and if I tried to keep them separate, it would take all of my time. So, in my sadness and happiness, I thank you, God! Lead me on the right path, for I am full of gratitude, and glad to be sitting in this room with you. Amen.

—Otto, age 94

Passage

Jesus said, "Remember, I am with you always, to the end of the age."
—Matthew 28:20

Perspective

To give thanks in our present state of sadness and happiness, as Otto does, reminds us that our joys and sorrows are intertwined. It is one thing to affirm this intellectually but quite another to live into its bittersweet truth over the span of a life.

Often our grief is over a joy we once relished but is now lost to us. Having loved deeply, we grieve in the same measure. When what we've cherished is no longer ours to enjoy, we are freshly acquainted with the gracious nature of what we once took for granted. In time, a deep sorrow may be the doorway to a fresh and unanticipated joy. Then again, sometimes a welcome happening sets the stage for an unexpected and unwelcome sorrow. The full cup of any life holds a blend of experiences, both pleasant and painful!

Longlife experience increases our capacity to give genuine thanks for this mix of sadness and happiness, for we have come to recognize how they are so intimately connected. As Otto's comment suggests, the inclusive embrace of gratitude has a way of opening our hearts in the immediate moment, where Holy Presence is sitting in the room with us. Amen.

Practice

Imagine that God, in whatever form is meaningful to you, is sitting in the room with you. Share a sadness and a happiness that have been intertwined in your life, and then give thanks.

Prayer

Loving God, may I find a settled peace in your presence. Let me be with you.

Up to Me?

*It's hard for me to get adjusted here. I keep wondering if it will
ever be any different, and if it is up to me to make it that way.*

—Patrick, age 75

Passage

You shall not oppress a resident alien; you know the heart of an alien, for you
were aliens in the land of Egypt.

—Exodus 23:9

Perspective

When adjusting to new life circumstances, we get a taste of what it feels like
to be an alien. We may ask, "Who will I be in this new place?" New to a community, we may wonder whether what we have to give will be noticed and
valued. Asking, as Patrick does, "Will it ever be any different?" is the start of
discerning what our role is in adapting to a new setting. This question invites
us to consider what initiatives are up to us.

For example, we may risk a friendly overture toward someone with
whom we'd like to be acquainted. What we can't make happen is receiving
the response we desire from that person. Cultivating an awareness of what

we can and cannot make happen keeps us in touch with the serendipity of relationship.

When a positive, reciprocal bond is made, it's because both persons stepped out in faith with no certain guarantee that their risk-taking would bear fruit. Remembering this, we can thank God for those who risk relationship with us and for the communities whose web of connection supports us.

Practice

How might the Holy Spirit be speaking to you through Patrick's question: "Will it ever be any different, and is it up to me to make it that way?"

Prayer

*God of pilgrimage, as you are with me on the journey from strangeness
to welcome inclusion, let me risk joining others on that same journey.*

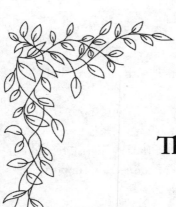

The School of Life

I grow every day. Things I wouldn't have accepted years ago, I accept now. I've learned acceptance—so it isn't so bad. I've learned from my mistakes too.

—Caroline, age 93

Passage

Jesus said, "Blessed are the meek, for they will inherit the earth."

—Matthew 5:5

Perspective

Life is often compared to a school in which we learn lessons of the heart, such as forgiveness, compassion, and acceptance. To be a receptive learner, it helps to focus less on what we already know and to exhibit curiosity about what we don't. A character in Barbara Kingsolvers's novel *The Poisonwood Bible* says it this way: "I've seen how you can't learn anything when you're trying to look like the smartest person in the room."[20]

The word *humility* is built on the same root word as the soil word *humus*. Thus, we might imagine humility as a down-to-earth soul space that lies between two distorted ways of being—prideful inflation and punctured deflation. Humility is neither arrogant nor self-abasing. Secure in God's love and forgiveness, we can be down-to-earth and our right size in the sacred space of humility. There we honestly can be puzzled about our behavior and ready to learn from our mistakes.

One of Jesus' beatitudes calls the meek "blessed." Perhaps that's because when we're humble, we can more readily receive God's blessing and let God bring blessing to the world through us. Embracing each day as opportunity for continued growth is one way to find purpose and be a blessing. In this way we are, indeed, lifelong learners.

Practice

Witness and thank God for opportunities to learn today. Create a personal gesture, such as placing a fingertip on your belly button or touching your index finger to your thumb. When you catch yourself in a puffed up or deflated state of mind, use that gesture to remind you to return to your right size.

Prayer

O God, prune and restore me to my right size. Keep me rooted and grounded in you, so I might branch out into a life of blessing.

In Our Being

God, I'm not able to do much physically, and I wonder how I'll be judged by you. God, you're supposed to love everybody, so perhaps you are forgiving me if I'm in a situation where I can't do as much as others, and I didn't create that situation.

—*Robert, age 80*

Passage

A woman named Martha welcomed [Jesus] into her home. She had a sister named Mary, who sat at the Lord's feet and listened to what he was saying. But Martha was distracted by her many tasks; so she came to him and asked, "Lord, do you not care that my sister has left me to do all the work by myself? Tell her then to help me." But the Lord answered her, "Martha, Martha, you are worried and distracted by many things; there is need of only one thing. Mary has chosen the better part, which will not be taken away from her."

—Luke 10:38-42

Perspective

In our society "doing" is treated almost as a nonmonetary form of net worth. Is it any wonder we easily imagine God as one who judges us for not doing enough? When we are in Martha mode, we can be drawn into comparative judgments about who's accomplishing more. Then we are apt to swing between self-righteousness about all that we're doing and self-recrimination when our life circumstances prevent us from doing as much.

Mary and Martha's story suggests that Jesus isn't interested in comparative busyness. He cares for both these women. Martha's industry may be born of the high value she places on offering hospitality, but she also uses her activity as a self-important platform from which to judge her sister's choices and assuage her own insecurities. Jesus invites Martha to draw from the deeper well of Holy Presence at which Mary finds refreshment. Whether we are active or still, the Holy Spirit beckons us to do the same.

Practice

Whether your being is expressing itself in activity or in quiet receptivity, imagine God as a divine, doting parent, lovingly beaming at you. Then imagine a compassionate core self that is extending that same unconditional acceptance to all of who you are.

Prayer

O God, since you brought me into being before I could do much of anything, help me trust that you bless my being, whether I am active or still.

Life Worth Living

I'm glad I was present when one of our men died. By talking face-to-face, it made him look brighter and more hopeful. I went to his bedside and put my hand in his just to be there. What makes life worth living is that we can give the gift of love. We're like a mirror; we're here to reflect love to others.

—Gregory, age 87

Passage

Jesus said, "I give you a new commandment, that you love one another. Just as I have loved you, you also should love one another. By this everyone will know that you are my disciples, if you have love for one another."

—John 13:34-35

Perspective

Finding purpose for living is something we wrestle with at every stage of life. What's meaningful to us in an earlier season may not suit us in a later season. This wrestling may prove even more intense when losing powers we've spent years acquiring and honing. Though diminished in his own physical strength, Gregory found meaning and purpose "just to be there" holding the hand of his dying friend.

Aside from breathing, brain activity, and a beating heart, the ability to give and receive love is a vital sign of life—a mark of our membership in the human family and the family of God. In loving and letting ourselves be loved by God and others, we discover purpose more profound and transcendent than personal survival. We find a continuing reason for being when we take a role in being God's love through supportive presence and compassionate acts.

Practice

Remember a "just to be there" moment in your life that left you feeling glad to have been there for someone who needed you. Celebrate the ways that God works through you as a conduit to express love.

Prayer

As you are ever with me, and I am with you, so may I be there for others, and let them be there for me.

Who's Responsible and Why?

God, I was taught that Jesus carried the cross for me, but it seems that some of us end up carrying the cross too. Why is this? Is the cross I'm carrying because I did something wrong, or because I was chosen? Did I bring bad things on myself, or did they just happen? Who's responsible and why?

—*Anthony, age 91*

Passage

Do not fear, for I have redeemed you;
    I have called you by name, you are mine.
When you pass through the waters, I will be with you;
    and through the rivers, they shall not overwhelm you;
when you walk through fire you shall not be burned,
    and the flame shall not consume you.

—*Isaiah 43:1-2*

Perspective

When we go through hard times, questions occur, like the ones Anthony asks. Humans try to keep painful and disruptive things from happening again by figuring out why they happened in the first place. In finding reasons for our difficulties, we feel more in control and sometimes discover ways to minimize future catastrophes.

In New Testament times, it was common to attribute suffering to the sins of the sufferer or those of their parents. But when asked about the "why" of someone's suffering, Jesus doesn't always chalk it up to behavioral causes. (See John 9:1-3.) Just as we recognize differing causes for suffering, so Jesus discerns particularities in each situation that inform his response. (See Luke 13:4-5.)

Jesus remarks that the weather does not discriminate. God "makes his sun rise on the evil and on the good, and sends rain on the righteous and the unrighteous" (Matt. 5:45). He seems to be suggesting that some weals and woes have little to do with whether one lives rightly. Instead, they are the natural lot of embodied, mortal creatures living on God's earth. For example, the same rain that ruins an outdoor wedding may be happily greeted by the farmer whose crops are parched. In a web of interdependent life forms, the suffering and death of one life form provides space or nourishment to another.

There is an inherent mystery in some kinds of suffering and no clear way to make cause-and-effect sense of it. If we instantly wrestle a reason why from some happenings, we may do emotional and ethical injustice to ourselves or others. Though God never promised we would be spared suffering, God has promised to be with us in it.

Practice

For what suffering in your life might you want to be more accountable? For what suffering in your life have you unfairly blamed yourself because you've found it difficult to sit with the mystery of that suffering?

Prayer

O God, help me discern the difference between suffering for which I am responsible and the mystery of suffering that makes no sense. Be beside me in all my troubles.

A Lot of Ground to Cover

It's a big, wide world out there, but some things I'm just not able to do anymore. But no matter my losses, I do what I can with whatever I have left. I try to do the best I can, and it's a lot of ground to cover.

—Larry, age 82

Passage

Three times I appealed to the Lord about this, that it would leave me, but he said to me, "My grace is sufficient for you, for power is made perfect in weakness." So, I will boast all the more gladly of my weaknesses, so that the power of Christ may dwell in me.

—2 Corinthians 12:8-9

Perspective

In this world of possibilities, each season of life presents us with new sets of limits. Those limits close the door on some possibilities while opening the door to others. Before we begin discovering possibilities within those new limits, we may experience inner turmoil as we go through a natural range of feelings about the losses we've suffered.

Reverend Greta Crosby, author and Unitarian Universalist minister, observes, "Loss makes artists of us all as we weave new patterns in the fabric of our lives."[21] It may seem a stretch to think of adjusting to losses as an artistic endeavor. Yet compelling art is often realized within limits imposed by environmental conditions, materials, and the skill of the artist. A fine artist is aware and respectful of such limits and makes creative use of them.

New limits invite us to identify fresh sources of meaning and purpose compatible with our altered circumstances. Limits also spur us to discover novel ways of getting our needs met, forging new neural pathways. In this endeavor we are co-creators with God. Doing the best we can within our limits is an exercise in artistic resourcefulness. As Larry says, "It's a lot of ground to cover."

Practice

What are some ways you see yourself as a collaborating creator with God in your current situation of limitation?

Prayer

God of possibilities, help me to be my artistic best with all I have. Working with me, release your creative power that I might make something of beauty within my limits and capacities.

Second-Guessing

Sometimes I wonder if things would have turned out differ-ently. I think, Maybe if I'd done this or that. *In hindsight it's always easier to see what I might have done differently. It's the not knowing what would have happened if I'd done otherwise that can drive me crazy.*

—*Frank, age 85*

Passage

For surely I know the plans I have for you, says the LORD, plans for your welfare and not for harm, to give you a future with hope. Then when you call upon me and come and pray to me, I will hear you. When you search for me, you will find me; if you seek me with all your heart.

—Jeremiah 29:11-13

Perspective

How easy it is to imagine things might have turned out better, had we made different choices! We say to ourselves and to one another: "if only," "would've," "could've," "should've." Exodus 16:2-3 tells us that as the Hebrews wander in Sinai's wilderness they reconsider their choice to flee Egypt for freedom.

They wonder aloud if slavery is preferable to the uncertainties of their present situation.

Evaluative hindsight has been useful to humanity as a way to reflect on choices and then make better choices. Hindsight can also result in anxiety and depression if we get bogged down in how things might have been different. Retrospective second-guessing delays our acceptance and readiness to work with what is and to accept our present circumstances peacefully.

When our best-laid plans take us places we haven't anticipated, it helps to recall that God's promise is to give us a future with hope. While what life deals us may be experienced as hurtful and harmful in human terms, nothing can cancel God's promise of a future with hope. That future hope may simply be that our life experiences intensify our growing sense of union with God and God's purposes in the world.

Practice

Notice when you are second-guessing your past choices. Then come back to the present to appreciate some aspect of the beauty of how things are.

Prayer

God who makes a way out of no way, free me from wallowing in what might have been. When the plans you have for me are only known to you, grant me patience as I wait for your promised "future with hope."

A Regular Beginner

No matter how grown up I am, I still come across times when I feel like a regular beginner. In making a new beginning, I draw on my past experiences, for they've equipped me to deal with new starts.

—George, age 96

Passage

The steadfast love of the LORD never ceases,
    his mercies never come to an end;
they are new every morning;
    great is your faithfulness.

—Lamentations 3:22-23

Perspective

We easily can identify with persons who are on the first day of a new job. Their eagerness to perform well and their anxiety about "getting it right" is apparent. Reminding newbies that there's only one first day on the job helps them relax and trust that they'll eventually catch on. To become competent, most beginners need to be dependent for a time. As beginners, how grateful we are when seasoned mentors assist us in learning the ropes!

Whenever we wade into newness, we gain valuable experience that helps us face future unknowns. Geographical moves, travel, and new jobs provide such opportunities. We face future unknowns in raising children or starting over in new communities with no guarantees of how things will turn out. These many acts of trust across the life cycle can be seen as opportunities to place our faith in the God who gives us a lifetime of opportunities.

Past experiences of beginning anew serve as reassuring touchstones when, in life's later season, we undergo novel experiences. Even those who are dying can feel like beginners in an intriguing and mysterious process. God's sustenance for us at such a time may include hospice personnel who regularly accompany others in their last days. They can serve as valuable end-of-life travel guides as we make this transition. If in our ending is our beginning, then to die is yet another act of trust in God's provision in life, in death, and beyond.

Practice

Notice moments today when you feel like a "regular beginner." If you see someone else showing signs of being a bewildered beginner, offer him or her an encouraging word.

Prayer

O God, be my divine travel guide as I start each new day's journey. Give me the open, curious, and receptive mind of "a regular beginner."

Not Alone

I used to think, What am I going to do all by myself? *But loneliness works itself out. It's a walk through dark wilderness. You can't see your way, but the way comes. There's so much that goes on, but when you quiet yourself down, you don't feel alone. You feel that somebody's there, and though so many who you've loved are gone, you're not alone.*

—*Althea, age 88*

Passage

[The Lord] sustained [Jacob] in a desert land,
    in a howling wilderness waste;
he shielded him, cared for him,
    guarded him as the apple of his eye.

—Deuteronomy 32:10

Perspective

The writer of Deuteronomy recounts how God tenderly protects the people of Israel when they are in dire straits. The nature of God's love for this people is compared to the doting, devoted love a parent might have for a favorite child.

When those dear to us have died and no longer provide us with the comfort of physical companionship, it may feel as if we are stumbling in a wilderness where it's hard to get our bearings. The noisy howl of our fears can leave us feeling even more disoriented and lonely. As Althea suggests, quieting down puts us in a more receptive state. There we may sense the continuing spiritual presence of our deceased loved ones. In quietness we attune to God's presence with us, as well as God's appreciative love for us, both as individuals and also as people.

Practice

As a way of quieting yourself, pay attention as you inhale and exhale over a period of a minute. If anxious thoughts bubble up, gently redirect your attention back to the breath. After doing this gentle breathing for a minute, do ten repetitions of this simple breath prayer, below.

Prayer

On the inhale: *breathe in me*
On the exhale: *breath of God*
At the end of the ten repetitions, say the Lord's Prayer. But when you get to the line: "Give us this day our daily . . ." substitute the word *breath* for the usual word *bread*.

Communing

What brings order and meaning? Sometimes communing with God and nature is the only way we can make sense of the challenges we have to face.

—Barbara, age 85

Passage

[Jesus said,] "For the bread of God is that which comes down from heaven and gives life to the world." [The crowd] said to him, "Sir, give us this bread always."

—John 6:33-34

Perspective

When Jesus' friends gather around the Passover table, Jesus gives them assurance of God's presence to carry them through the trials they will soon face. He does this by inviting them to experience God's presence through eating, an activity as familiar as their own bodies, a needful activity for human beings. Using two foods common to his culture, Jesus compares bread and wine to his body and blood. (See Luke 22:19-20.) Jesus invites his disciples to feed on God's presence and know that Jesus is with them at that pregnant moment in time.

In comparing his life force to common foodstuffs, Jesus offers a related invitation to disciples past and present. He invites his followers to take nourishment from a holy presence that is both in us and with us. His is a presence that is not only the holy lifeblood of the entire creation but also as close to our home in the body as the food from the natural world that renews us daily.

Whether we woke up this morning feeling weary or well, powerless or energized, we can come to the feast of this day ready to receive God's presence in communion with nature outside our window, in the simplest acts that maintain life in our bodies, and in the conversation we share with others. In each day God grants us may we discover an unexpected holy meal that feeds our deepest hungers.

Practice

Imagine this day as a holy supper through which you might taste God's presence in various forms. What would you identify as the appetizer, the main course, the dessert?

Prayer

Grant me a hearty appetite for communion with you and a nose for the enticing aroma of your presence in my daily life. In my heart let me feast on you by faith with thanksgiving.

Go Ahead and Ask

You can't hide from God how you want things to be, so if you want something, go ahead and ask. Who knows what you'll receive? You do get things in response to prayer. You do get answers. God will bless you, but the blessing may not be exactly the way you want it.

—Georgine, age 78

Passage

Then [Jesus] withdrew from [the disciples] about a stone's throw, knelt down, and prayed, "Father, if you are willing, remove this cup from me; yet, not my will but yours be done."

—Luke 22:41-42

Perspective

One way we hide from God is to pretend to not want what we want. In Gethsemane, Jesus does not hide but models full exposure before God. He's upfront about his druthers. We too are free to reveal to God our desired outcomes. Just as God's ways are not our ways, how things actually unfold may not resemble the answer for which we prayed: our spouse may not be cured of cancer, our ego's cravings may not be satisfied, we may remain chronically ill. Sometimes answers, even blessings, may come but not always in the way we'd envisioned.

Though our prayers may not result in wished-for answers, prayer and the mystery of unanswered prayer transform us. They change how we understand and relate to God and others. They lead us to contemplate and then surrender to the possibility of broader purposes that lie beyond our narrow vision.

In praying "not my will, but yours be done," Jesus models a willingness to give way to the mystery of divine purpose.[22] This willingness is an act of radical trust. His ego, interest, and desire for personal survival are ceded to the One he trusts more than life itself. May we too find such a capacity for gracious surrender as we approach our life's end.

Practice

Imagine your life as an ongoing prayer that includes both an honest admission of your willful desire and a humble willingness to make way for God.

Prayer

I confess, God, that there is much I want for myself and for those I love. May I grow in willingness to align my will with yours and trust your wisdom in the outcomes.

O God, Why?

I'm not quite as patient and I'll tell you why,
My time's getting shorter. O God, why?
But if I should hurry, I'm liable to trip,
My mind's not the same, it's starting to slip.
So many things I can no longer do,
So much of me I can no longer use—O God, why?

—Peter, age 91

Passage

My God, my God, why have you forsaken me?
    Why are you so far from helping me, from the words of my groaning?
O my God, I cry by day, but you do not answer;
    and by night, but find no rest.

—Psalm 22:1-2

Perspective

To live with unanswerable questions is to be human. Quoting the words of this psalm from the cross, Jesus reminds us that we are in good company when we ask, "O God, why?" For such questions there are seldom satisfying answers. We may or may not find meaning in seemingly senseless things that befall us. If we offer easy answers to others' suffering, we may be making only ourselves feel better rather than coming alongside them with true support.

As we accumulate losses along our length of days, doubts may arise. Doubt does not reflect an absence of trust, nor does its presence disqualify us as a person of faith. Were we absolutely certain about why things happen as they do, what need would we have of faith? Rather, doubt and faith are two complementary ways of wrestling with unanswerable questions. If creatively engaged, doubts beckon our faith out of an immature infancy to engage the nitty-gritty of real life. For its part, faith tempers doubt with gratitude, hope, and humility.[23]

As doubt's intrepid traveling companion, faith trusts—despite evidence to the contrary—that a loving God is at the beating heart of this mystifying world in which we find ourselves.

Practice

How might your "O God, why?" questions serve as opportunities to deepen your trust in God in the face of life's unanswerable questions?

Prayer

Wrestle with me in the arena of my doubts and questions, God. Release me to inhabit the unknown, so I might dwell with you in wonder and abandon.

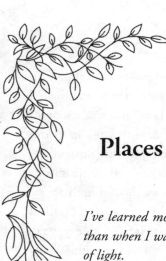

Places of Darkness and Light

I've learned more in my stay on this planet in my later years than when I was young. I've gone from a dark place to a place of light.

—*Victor, age 81*

Passage

For now we see in a mirror, dimly, but then we will see face to face. Now I know only in part; then I will know fully, even as I have been fully known.

—1 Corinthians 13:12

Perspective

The experience of going from darkness to a place of light is as primal as birth itself. A baby knows no other reality than the darkness of the womb until it emerges into the light. At the other end of the age spectrum, we don't fully appreciate how significantly cataracts have dimmed our vision until they've been removed, and our view of the world is clarified.

This is also true when it comes to spiritual vision. We're unaware of the extent to which we've been living in a dimly lit reality until we find ourselves in a brighter place. As we shed illusions about what life is about, we naturally gain clearer sight while becoming more illumined from within. With honest hindsight, we see more clearly how some of our behaviors and attitudes have obscured our view of life, ourselves, and others.

To see face-to-face is to have the "eyes" of our heart enlightened. (See Ephesians 1:17-18.) For most of us, the opening of our spiritual eyes is an ongoing process that spans a lifetime of learning how to live and love. It may not be until we die that we'll see clearly, face-to-face. Still, even now, our faith invites us to trust that the face we will see will be the face of God.

Practice

How have the more shadowy and dimly lit places of your life served as wombs preparing you to emerge into a place of greater light and clarified spiritual sight?

Prayer

God, the darkness and the light are alike to you. Be my vision! Whether my sight is cloudy or clear, may I see the world through your merciful eyes.

Where Are You, God?

Where are you, God? Where are you right now? Sometimes my body hurts. What's happening to me, God?

—Paul, age 86

Passage

Why, O Lord, do you stand far off?
Why do you hide yourself in times of trouble?

—Psalm 10:1

Perspective

The feeling that God is watching over us waxes and wanes, ebbs and flows, comes and goes. When things are going well in our lives, we're less apt to lament that God seems distant. Just as children tend to equate their well-being with the presence of their trusted, responsive parents, so we tend to equate things going well for us with a sense of God's consoling presence.

When we feel distressed by what is happening in our lives or our bodies, it can be much harder to trust that God is present. People of faith have debated over whether it is God who distances from us, or whether it is we who have distanced ourselves from God. In either case, we deeply grieve the loss of a sense of God's presence, and that grieving itself is a process. Such a loss also presents an opportunity to strengthen our capacity to trust God—to walk by faith and not solely by the consolations that come with a palpable sense of God's presence.

Through parental comings and goings, children learn to trust in their parents' constancy. Children begin to grasp that their parents continue to exist somewhere, out there, even when they are not physically present.[24] Similarly, through personal experiences of God's presence and absence, we learn to assure ourselves that God continues to exist whatever our personal capacity is to feel God-with-us on any given day.

Practice

Reflect on how your experiences of God's presence and absence have deepened your capacity to trust God through times when God's accompaniment is not apparent.

Prayer

Elusive God, when you seem far off, may I imagine you as somewhere out there, soon to return. When I search for you in vain, may I imagine that you lie closer than the skin that sheaths my aging frame. Though you cannot be pinned down, accept my pining for you as evidence of our everlasting bond.

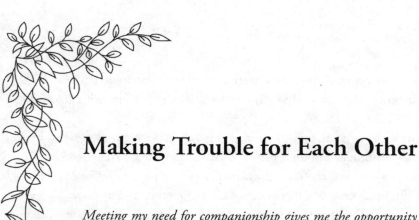

Making Trouble for Each Other

Meeting my need for companionship gives me the opportunity to get together with others, which is good for me and for them. It also gives us the opportunity to make trouble for each other. What brings trouble is conflict between neighbors, but salvation from such trouble is respect of neighbors.

—*Conrad, age 83*

Passage

Cain said to his brother Abel, "Let us go out to the field." And when they were in the field, Cain rose up against his brother Abel, and killed him. Then the LORD said to Cain, "Where is your brother Abel?" He said, "I do not know; am I my brother's keeper?"

—Genesis 4:8-9

Perspective

Conrad reflects on how the need for companions can bear good fruit, even while being a potential source of friction. In congregate care settings, persons inhabit close quarters with strangers whose companionship they did not choose. Sometimes new and nourishing relationships spring up, while at other times personal habits never imagined may annoy others, cause problems, and create conflict. Respect for ourselves and neighbors leads us to seek mutual compromise, and if need be, the mediation of an unbiased third party.

Our human tendency to compare our circumstances with someone else's can also be a breeding ground for trouble. When comparing how his offering was received to the reception given to his brother's, Cain was miffed. Then he allowed that annoyance to develop into a murderous rage.

Perhaps our roommate receives more visitors, underscoring our lack of them. We may be bed-bound while our friend is relatively mobile. In warning us of the emotional toll of comparisons, one unknown sage quipped: "Compare and despair!" When we respect ourselves as God respects us, we honor our own unique journey by changing the things we can while accepting the inalterable differences between our path and our neighbor's.

Practice

Find a mutually respectful way to compromise today. When you catch yourself in a comparison that kindles your anger or despair, imagine God whispering in your ear, "You are enough, for you are mine."

Prayer

Giving God, be my encouraging "enough" when I am feeling "less than." Guide me in making mutual compromises that honor my God-given dignity and the dignity of my neighbor.

Why Am I Here?

When I look up at the universe, I say: "Why am I here out of all this? There must be something in me that needs to contribute."

—Mae, age 89

Passage

When I look at your heavens, the work of your fingers,
    the moon and the stars that you have established;
what are human beings that you are mindful of them,
    mortals that you care for them?
Yet you have made them a little lower than God,
    and crowned them with glory and honor.

—Psalm 8:3-5

Perspective

Our busy, anxious minds can be quieted in a moment of beholding a sunset, a moonrise, a bird on the wing, or a weathered human face. Sometimes it's sufficiently meaningful to gratefully witness the vast universe in which we participate. Sometimes the amazement of being alive seems purpose enough. But such awestruck beholding can also lead us to further contemplate our reason for being. With the psalmist, we ask, "What is our unique contribution as human beings?"

As we age, we may doubt our capacity to contribute, but the desire to do so remains. It can be a challenge to trust that graces flowing from our simple presence are received by others. The glory with which we are crowned may be apparent to others but not to us.

The glory of Christ radiates from his courageous, authentic, and loving way of being in the world. In his living and dying, Jesus opens himself to being transformed by God. His resurrection is evidence of that metamorphosis. No matter how timeworn our body, in living a life of faith we too are being transformed through living and dying. We contribute by being an image through whom God can be seen. The transparent radiance of our being may be gift enough to others, and evidence of the work of God's hands.

Practice

How might God be using your beneficial presence in ways beyond your knowing? How might you feel differently about yourself if you trusted that God is working through you?

Prayer

O God, though the glory of my spiritual metamorphosis is hidden from me, continue to transform me. Though I may be clueless, use my very being to contribute until the day my life is totally surrendered into yours.

SCRIPTURE INDEX

Hebrew Scriptures

Genesis 1:16-19	Sweet Mystery of Life 72
Genesis 1:26	Baking a New Beginning 60
Genesis 1:31–2:1	That's Good 30
Genesis 2:18	Worth the Risk? 53
Genesis 4:8b-9	Making Trouble for Each Other 116
Genesis 33:10	Seeing God in People's Faces 74
Exodus 16:2-3	Second-Guessing 100
Exodus 16:13-21	Not Digestible! 68
Exodus 23:9	Up to Me? 88
Deuteronomy 32:10	Not Alone 104
2 Chronicles 36:19-20	Durable and Portable 32
Psalm 8:3-5	Why Am I Here? 118
Psalm 10:1	Where Are You, God? 114
Psalm 16:11	The Path of Life 84
Psalm 19: 1-2	Medicinal Powers 44
Psalm 22:1-2	O God, Why? 110
Psalm 23:1-3	Comfort and Refresh Us 58
Psalm 46:10	Quieting the Crazy Things 50
Psalm 71:9	Can Less Be More? 26
Psalm 90:12	Quality Living 54
Psalm 90:13-14	Another Day of Fun and Love 70
Psalm 90:16-17	Carry On! 20
Psalm 118:24	Dread and Delight 76

Psalm 139:7-10   Wherever We Go 16
Proverbs 1:8-9   Things We Can Teach 62
Proverbs 17:22   A Winking God 56
Isaiah 40:29-31   The Gift of a Lift 78
Isaiah 43:1b-2   Who's Responsible and Why? 96
Isaiah 49:14-16a   Remember Me 82
Jeremiah 29:11-13   Second Guessing 100
Ezekiel 11:19-20   Tough and Tender 64
Lamentations 3:22-23   A Regular Beginner 102

New Testament

Matthew 5:4   Worth the Risk? 52
Matthew 5:5   The School of Life 90
Matthew 5:45   Who's Responsible and Why? 96
Matthew 7:24-27   Checking the Foundations 24
Matthew 12:46-50   Baking a New Beginning 60
Matthew 13:45-46   Not Digestible! 68
Matthew 18:20   Hidden in Plain Sight 38
Matthew 28:20b   Sitting with God 86
Mark 1:40-41   Response of Caring 66
Mark 12:31   Is This the Same Person? 40
Mark 12:30-31   I Love Myself! 48
Luke 10:27-28   Checking the Foundations 24
Luke 10:38b-42   In Our Being 92
Luke 13:4-5   Who's Responsible and Why? 96
Luke 22:19-20   Communing 106
Luke 22:41-42   Go Ahead and Ask 108
John 6:33-34   Communing 106
John 9:1-3   Who's Responsible and Why? 96
John 13:34-35   Life Worth Living 94
John 14:6a   Finding New Ways 22
Acts 17:27b-28   Acting for God 80
Romans 8:22-25   Already. . .Not Yet 34
1 Corinthians 13:1-2   Love or Nothing 36

1 Corinthians 13:12 — Places of Darkness and Light 112

2 Corinthians 12:8-9 — A Lot of Ground to Cover 98

Ephesians 1:17-18 — Places of Darkness and Light 112

Hebrews 2:11 — Baking A New Beginning 60

Hebrews 11:1 — Expecting Small Miracles 18

James 1:19a — A Good Listener 28

1 Thessalonians 5:18 — Desert Grit and Gratitude 42

1 John 4:12, 16 — I Love Myself! 48

1 John 4:8, 16 — The Path of Life 84

NOTES

1. D. W. Winnicott, *Playing and Reality* (Tavistock Publications Ltd., 1971; New York: Routledge, 1989), 138-139. Citation refers to the Routledge edition.

2. James Weldon Johnson, *God's Trombones* (New York: Viking Penguin, 1955), 17.

3. William Wordsworth, "Ode: Intimations of Immortality from Recollections of Early Childhood," in *Introduction to Literature: Poems*, eds. Lynn Altenbernd and Leslie L. Lewis (New York: The Macmillian Company, 1963), 238.

4. Bernhard W. Anderson, *Understanding the Old Testament,* 4th ed. (Englewood Cliffs, NJ: Prentice-Hall, 1986), 448–50.

5. Charles Dickens, *Our Mutual Friend* (New York: Alfred A. Knopf, Inc., 1907), 671.

6. John Bowlby, *Attachment and Loss, Volume 11: Separation* (The Tavistock Institute of Human Relations, 1973), 30–31.

7. Joshua Liebman, *Peace of Mind* (New York: Simon and Schuster, 1946), 89.

8. Viktor E. Frankl, *Man's Search for Meaning: An Introduction to Logotherapy,* 4th ed. (Boston: Beacon Press, 1992), 74–75.

9. Hafiz, "Two Giant Fat People," in *The Gift: Poems by Hafiz The Great Sufi Master,* trans. Daniel Ladinsky (New York: Penguin Group, 1999), 199.

10. Don Mitchell, *The Souls of Lambs* (Boston: Houghton Mifflin Company, 1979), 104.

11. Mitchell MacCulloch, *Christianity: The First Three Thousand Years* (New York: The Penguin Group, 2009), 226–27.

12. Rollin McCraty, *Science of the Heart*: Volume 2 (Boulder Creek, CA: Heart Math Institute, 2015), 164–65.

13. Anderson, *Understanding the Old Testament,* 4th ed., 85.

14. "The Shorter Catechism," in *The Constitution of the Presbyterian Church (U.S.A.), Part I: Book of Confessions* (Louisville, KY: Office of the General Assembly, 1983), 7.001.

15. Herbert Victor, "Ah! Sweet Mystery of Life," lyrics Rida Johnson Young (New York: M. Witmark & Sons, 1910).

16. Daniela Breitman, "Today in Science: Comet Hale-Bopp," in EarthSky, April 1, 2016, https://earthsky.org/space/this-date-in-science-comet-hale-bopp.

17. Sandy Podulka, Ronald W. Rohrbaugh, Jr., and Rick Bonney, eds., *Handbook of Bird Biology,* 2nd ed. (Ithaca, NY: Cornell Lab of Ornithology, 2004), 5.10–5.11.

18. Søren Kierkegaard, "The Concept of Anxiety," in *The Essential Kierkegaard*, Howard V. Hong and Edna H. Hong (Princeton, NJ: Princeton University Press, 1995), 150.

19. "The Prayer of Boethius," in *The Oxford Book of Prayer,* George Appleton, ed. (Oxford, UK: Oxford University Press, 1985), 7.

20. Barbara Kingsolver, *The Poisonwood Bible: A Novel* (New York: HarperCollins, 1998), 229.

21. Greta Crosby, *Tree and Jubilee* (Boston: Unitarian Universalist Association, 1982).

22. Gerald May, *Will and Spirit: A Contemplative Psychology* (New York: HarperCollins, 1982), 5-6.

23. Gary Henry, "A Faith Strengthened by Doubt," in "The Expository Files," Warren E. Berkley and Jon W. Quinn, eds. Accessed April 5, 2019. http://www.bible.ca/ef/topical-a-faith-strengthened-by-doubt.htm.

24. Winnicott, *Playing and Reality*, 106–09.

ABOUT THE AUTHOR

Susan Carol Scott is self-employed in private practice as a spiritual director, retreat leader, and supply preacher. An ordained clergyperson in the United Church of Christ, Susan is authorized by her judicatory for specialized ministry as a healthcare chaplain and spiritual director. She is board certified with the Association of Professional Chaplains.